Sparks Of Light

A Teaching Story About The Circle Of Life

Christine Word

Illustrated by Cayla Zeek

Sparks Of Light

A Teaching Story About

The Circle of Life

_____

Christine Word

WORD
p r e s s

Lafayette, Louisiana 2016

Sparks of Light

for

Laila

Dear Parents, Grandparents,
And all those who care for children,

My little granddaughter was having a hard time dealing with a death in the family. Her sadness created in me a desire to help her see this part of life in a way that would comfort her. Showing a higher perspective of who we are and what we're doing here is my intention.

I hope this story of our spiritual nature will inspire your own teachings with your children, grandchildren or those in your care, about the greatest of mysteries - the circle of life.

Christine Word

"*L*ook," said Little Angel, "here comes another one!"

Little Angel pointed to a bright spark of light falling from

the night sky. The other angel saw it too and smiled.

"Tell me again," said Little Angel, all excited.

"Tell me the story of the sparks!"

"**W**ell," said Beautiful Angel gathering up Little Angel

in its soft white light, "I'll show you this time so you can

remember."

And suddenly the sky seemed to open

and here's what Little Angel saw:

Music stirred the darkness and bright colors

swirled around. In the middle, a strong force grew.

"Its name is ' Love'," said Beautiful Angel.

As Little Angel watched the show in the sky,

it saw how awesome is the one called 'Love'

and that It is All there is because it keeps everything

within Itself. All the colors were there and the music

made the sounds of happiness.

Then the stirring got stronger and the music grew louder.

The colors flew off of Love like tiny sparks off a great bonfire.

Little Angel could tell that these Sparks are the same as Love

only smaller. They have a special place to go and special things

to do.

"And so, here comes another one," said Beautiful Angel.

Little Angel Smiled.

"*W*ow! What a great adventure they're having," exclaimed Little Angel.

It could see that all of the Sparks drifted down into sweet bundles called babies wrapped in their blankets and cared for by the people in their world.

*E*ach would have a part to play in their earth lives.

Just like putting on a costume, one becomes a mommy,

one, a mechanic, a fireman, a farmer, or a fisherman.

There's a doctor, and over there a truck driver,

a postman, a builder and a teacher.

There are daddies, nurses, explorers, scientists, grandpas,

and presidents of countries.

Some make music. Some write. Some paint.

Some sing. Some dance. All are helpers in their place.

*B*ut there's one big problem.

They have all forgotten they are Sparks of Light.

They think they are only their costumes.

So their real job is to remember.

It's like they fell into a dream when they came to Earth

and now they have to wake up.

The most important thing for all Sparks of Light

is to be their true selves...to be Love in this world.

*A*nd all through this time their angels follow behind,

keeping them connected to Love.

Then when their part in the play is over,

they can leave the costume and go home again.

In their bodies of Light, they soar like shooting

stars to where they began.

They join the ones who have
been waiting for them and watching over them.
And they wait for other Sparks to
join them there too.

This is your story.

It's a true story.

You are a Spark of Light.

You are a Spark of Love.

This is Life and it goes on and on

...in Love.

No End

"FOR IN THE BEGINNING GOD SAID, 'LET THERE BE LIGHT.'

YOU ARE ONE OF THOSE SPARKS OF LIGHT..."

-EDGAR CAYCE

(5367-1)

Christine Word is author of <u>Ghosts Along the Bayou</u> which started her mystical search and study of our spiritual nature. She offers presentations related to life purpose. She and her husband Duke raised five children and live in Lafayette, Louisiana, close-by their eight grandchildren. She can be reached at christineword33@gmail.com.

Cayla Zeek is an award-winning visual artist who pursues her passion for painting at her home studio in Lafayette. She exhibits her work in galleries throughout Louisiana. Her hand-drawn illustrations are available at her design business on matteashand.com and her paintings can be viewed at caylazeek.com.

Special Acknowledgment and Appreciation

goes to Sandra Sarr's Writers' Group in Breaux Bridge, Louisiana

for their enthusiasm and encouragement to publish this story

I wish to express gratitude for the eight special Sparks who share their Light with me:

Laila, Lucas, Branson, Brec, Christian, Maya, Wyatt, Allie and those yet to come.

www.ingramcontent.com/pod-product-compliance
Lightning Source LLC
Chambersburg PA
CBHW042102040426
42448CB00002B/109